It is, in these p Days, a suffici to have printe which has so boldly dared to doubt the Infallibility of Ministers, and to investigate the Justice and Policy of their Measures.

Joseph Gales, 'The Editor's Address',
Sheffield Register No 369, 27 June 1794.

When Joseph Gales was editing the *Register* his readers did not take newspapers for granted. Newspaper readers in the 1790s, and those who wrote for them, were still working out the boundaries of what a newspaper could or should do. By 1794 regional newspapers had only been around for a century or so: a blink of an eye for a form in literary history.

Printed news as we would recognise it only began to circulate in Britain around the middle of the 1600s, fuelled by a time of civil war. By the early 1700s there were local as well as national newspapers and they had begun to take a recognisable form. As the 1700s progressed, newspapers began to circulate across the country with greater ease, often moving from weekly to thrice-weekly and even (at first in London) a daily format. By 1794 your newspaper of choice had all of today's features in place: it would have a masthead, it would announce its price, its place and date of publication, and it would have local, national and international news divided into recognisable columns containing advertisements, letters, illustrations and so-forth.

Newspapers were also hard work: each line of text was typeset in movable lead blocks, set back-to-front by skilled printers who then had to ink each frame full of type and use a hand-powered press to make the print. The skills, the ink, the (taxed) paper: none of it was cheap, yet then as now a newspaper was disposable, out of date the moment it hit the streets. At the end of the 18th century newspaper proprietors made real money not from the cover price but from advertisements. That meant they had to print papers that people would pay to read: otherwise the advertisements would dry up and the paper would fail. This means that whatever Gales printed in the *Register* he thought people would want to read. He was not a lone ideologue, he was a businessman who needed to keep his readers and his advertisers in harmony.

That is one reason why these poems are so important: they represent not an abstract aesthetic ideal of what makes good poetry or a work of genius; this, rather, is the literature that real readers in Sheffield actually wanted to see in their weekly newspaper. If Gales got it wrong, he would go bust: a refreshing kind of literary criticism.

Newspapers appealed to and were bought by people who had the time and education to read them and the money to buy them. Such people cared about a world beyond their own front door. Newspapers offered an exciting, sometimes challenging, window on a world beyond people's everyday experiences and played a key role in defining a new phenomenon: public opinion. Open a copy of the *Register* to find reports of violence in Europe, suspicion of foreigners, distrust of politicians, anxiety about the economy and tax, arguments about religion, opinions about the latest fashion. It is much the same material as today, although we have had 300 years to get used to the idea of 'news', even to take it for granted. Just as today, so in 1794 the government – and the everyday reader – had to decide when and where to take matters seriously; to decide who to trust and what to fear; to decide who to ignore and what information to act upon. To make these choices was to become a member of an emerging British public. To hold and to test opinions amongst the community represented by the readers of the *Register* was to engage in a new and powerful sense of public identity. The *Register* brought the people of Sheffield together and connected Sheffield to the outside world; it was a remarkably powerful institution that shaped and challenged the self-understanding of its readers and so was watched closely by the government.

Hamish Mathison
Project Director

He whose voice called the universe into existence could have formed it in one moment, but he chose to complete his work in six days, and rested on the seventh, to teach man, whom he formed in his image, that every great, every arduous, every noble work must be the fruit, the reward, the crown, of persevering industry, and unwearied well-doing. Go on, therefore, friends of freedom, friends of mankind, go on, tyranny, despotism, and priest-craft, must fall with a crash that will astonish the universe, therefore, INVINCIBLE, go on—PROSPER—and triumph.

From a Letter by James Montgomery, *Sheffield Register* No 334, 25 October 1793.

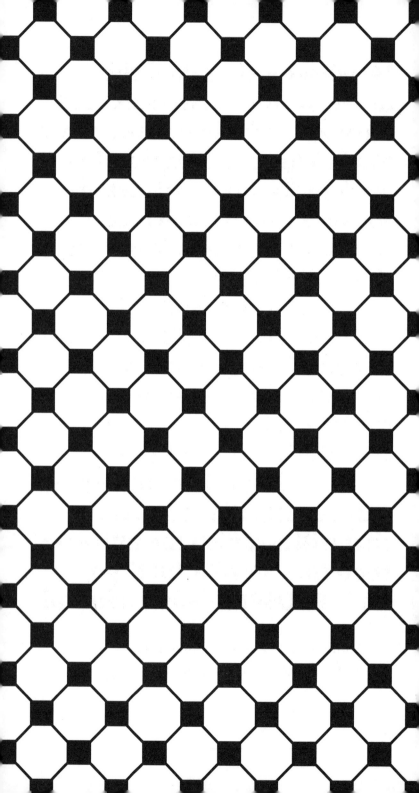

A Loyal Song

For the Tars of Old England, 1793
Tune 'Derry Down'

Come cheer up my boys, though the times are thought bad,
Though Pitt's at the Helm, and the Nation stark mad;
Yet since the War is declar'd as sure as a gun,
When we meet with Messieurs, we shall have some rare fun.

Derry down &c.

Some fools they complain of Tythes and Taxation,
Addressers have shewn they're good for the nation;
That the first are just Rights, the Church has decreed,
And if War we must have, our coffers must bleed.

Derry down &c.

As for honest John Bull, we may banish our fears,
His sharp Horns are cut off and likewise his Ears;
From his anger we then have nothing to dread,
He'll bear what you will from his tail to his Head.

Derry down &c.

The French in their Councils, expressly declare,
No concern will they have in an Offensive war;
But our Senate by *number* their arguments face,
And forbid us to trust such an infamous race.

Derry down &c.

The Dutch, who by treaty, might now our aid claim,
By their silence have shewn, War is not their Aim;
But in Slaughter and Bloodshed, we take such delight,
That in spite of their teeth we swear they shall fight.

Derry down &c.

As for what we may gain, or lose on this score,
Such as Commerce and Trade and twenty things more;
Our Rulers don't wish us to think of such things,
Tis enough if we fight for CHURCH, LORDS and KINGS.

Derry down &c.

On the Effects of Gold

Would you silence a Patriot committee,
Touch their lips with this magic wand;
Through country and senate and city,
Tis the lock and key of this land.

Take a piece of this same from your coffer,
Display to the voter your pelf;
And the wretch, having nothing to offer,
Will frugally sell you—HIMSELF.

'Tis a shot for the fowl of all feather,
A bait for the guts of all fish;
To this ever gudgeon will gather,
And plumpt, ready drest, in your dish.

If the booby, your pupil, so dull is,
He scarce can remember his name;
Yet his mouth it shall open like TULLY's,
When fed with a spoon of this same.

To a Rascal, a Bear, and a Blockhead,
Unconscious of mood or of tense,
This plastic receipt in his pocket,
Gives grace, figure and sense!

Old saints will for this sell their manuals;
O'er this, at your sovereign nod,
Old judges will skip like young spaniels,
And Cardinals kiss you this rod.

To study aught else is but nonsense;
From hence all Philosophy springs—
'Tis the Crown, Beauty, Cause and good Conscience,
Of—Priests, Ladies, Lawyers and Kings.

By C. B.

The Bull

A simile addressed to John Bull

Seest thou yon Bull?—how awful to behold,
Cast in great Nature's most stupendous mould!
Nature alone could form the grand design,
And soften Majesty with Beauty join.
He towers unrivalled Monarch of the Plain,
Strength every limb and fire in every vein!
Mark the brave brow, that bravest the bended sky,
The voice of thunder and the lightning Eye!
That voice which roused could awe the light away,
That Eye which fired could kindle Night to Day!
Yet wherefore, wherefore, O mysterious Heaven!
Was so much *strength* and so much *weakness* given?
He bows his passive neck—a slender string,
Confines his might and leads the savage King!
Tame he submits—till pestilential gore,
In baneful blasts repels him from the door,
Where slaughter lives—sudden he makes a stand,
Wild roll his Eyes, his Nostrils dire expand:
But e'er his *fears* his *courage* can awake,
Stones, Goads and Cudgels force him to the Stake;
There bound, the moaning Victim's left to wait
In agonizing pangs, his lingering fate!
   O! In that moment, darted through his frame,
Should sudden fury touch his powers to flame,
See, at one plunge, the uprooted post, the walls—
The unsupported roof—the fabric falls—
Death and Destruction, Terror and Dismay!
These rush before, and those attend his way!
Where'er he turns his dastard Butchers fly,
He desolates the Country with his Eye!
   BRITANNIA know thy strength! thy Rights regain,
When Britons *sue* shall Britons *sue* in vain?
But should the People's Voice their Rights *demand*?
The People's Voice! Which nothing can withstand!
Though steel'd against a weeping Nations tears
Tyrants are governed only by their fears—
For Freedom all the Nations look to thee;
Britannia speaks and bid the Universe be free!

By Musaeus
(Sheffield, 9 April 1793)

No Libel to Think

In a state of oppression, we'll *sigh* our complaints;
It may seal our destruction, to *tell out* our wants;
For we've freedom enough, while we've freedom to think.

We may speak (it is true) if we mind what we say;
But to *speak all we think,* will not suit in our day:
Tho' our tongues be cut out, or chain'd fast with this link,
Who dares say we're not free, while we've freedom to think?

They tell us our state is both perfect and pure,
The ills we point out do not want any cure;
To believe such a doctrine, our reason must sink;
So we'll think as we please, while we've freedom to think.

Can a man clothe his back, or eat his own bread?
Can he marry his wife, or bury his dead?
All such matters as these, will make his coin chink—
We can think of such things while we've freedom to think.

Can a man use his eyes, his hands, or his tongue,
But must pay for the services these members have done?
And yet more than all these are just on the brink;
What strange thoughts we have when we've freedom to think!

From the sole of the foot, to the crown of the head,
They stamp us, and tax us, both living and dead!
And yet at such hardship they wish us to wink;
But we cannot do this—while we've freedom to think.

When the sunshine of LIBERTY breaks on our sight,
The reform of abuses we'll claim as our RIGHT:
'The Friends of Reform' is the toast we will drink,
And we'll think of our Rights—*while we've Freedom to* THINK!

By T. G.
(Sheffield, 19 April 1793)

Lines

Supposed to be written by a young Lady of this Town, upon reading the following passage in our last paper: 'They poured upon our troops a shower of grape and musket shot that brought to the ground some of our bravest men'.

Then he is fallen! for he was brave!
My WILLY sinks among the dead!
His cold limbs press no friendly grave,
But night's damp winds blow round his head!

Fallen is my love! and low he lies!
Ah! had this cheek his pale cheek prest;
These fingers clos'd his fading eyes;
And claspt him to my faithful brest!

My WILLY's fallen! for he was brave!
Ah! Why my love was I not there!
Thy face with Sorrow's drops to leave,
And bathe thee with my fallen tear.

Yes, he was brave! and now lies low—
Heavens why am I so far away!
Why must I not the soft mould show
Upon my WILLY's lifeless clay!

He's fallen! He's fallen! for he was brave!
His limbs unbury'd yet remain:
Heaven grant the little boon I crave—
—Why ask the boon! 'tis all in vain,

To see that youth, who once was brave!
O'er his lov'd form to sit and weep;
And bid in peace his spirit sleep.

The Statesman's Soliloquy

Reform!—the Statesman cries, 'ye Powers forefend!
E'en from the word what horrors dire impend.
Reform! — ah! shield me from its searching eyes,
Aid me ye schemes, ye arts, ye subtlest lies;
E'en now, methinks, I feel its baneful pow'r,
Rush o'er my soul and ev'ry dream devour.
Asleep, awake, the chilling sound torments,
And starting Fancy still fresh pangs invents.
Tortures like these attend its dreaded name,
And madness as they pierce my sick'ning frame;
But should the Vision rob'd with power appear,
What sad detection must our actions fear!
What waste, confusion, treachery and bribes!
What shoals of Placemen, and what pension'd Tribes
Will then, forlorn, no more sweet spoil partake,
But grieve their bondsmen are at last awake!
Avert the plague, ye Gods! or if your rage
Must careless burn, til cool reform assuage;—
Defer it yet; alas! 'tis yet too soon
To crop any budding fortunes in their noon;
Give me yet one Septennial more to reap,
One more Septennial let the People sleep!'
—He ceas'd and hurrying to Stephen's Gate,
Finds still new cause to curse his pending fate.

By Libertior

The Observations of a Swine, on the Condition of his Fellow Creatures

Occasioned by the Lines which appear in the Register, of the 3rd inst. entitled 'Patriotism'.

Did 'Nature mean us to be slaves'
The property of fools and knaves?
Have we no claim or just pretense
To common rights and common sense?
Or, will you have say the Hand divine
Made some for Lords—the rest for Swine?
If this be fact, explain the cause
Why Swine must needs be ruled by laws?
Except we call their fate a law,
To eat dry husks and lay on straw,
And when they've fattened to be taken
And quarter'd into hams and bacon,
To satiate those who think it fit,
To eat the carcass bit by bit:—
Although ALL should not suffice,
Except our lot's a sacrifice,
'Twould be call'd Treason to repine!
Because, you know, we're only Swine!

We're only Swine!—how well it suits!
For shall putes may govern brutes;
And foolish men, in foolish things,
Oft act as well as foolish Kings:
Let SWINEHERD be the name for those,
Who lead the Nation by the nose,
And boast, that by a right divine,
They're ruling men:—no,—driving Swine!

We're only Swine!—think but what fun,
To see a Pig strut with his gun!
How fierce and terrible the fight,
To march large herds of Swine to fight!
The illustrious YORK, that noble Peer,
How famous must his name appear!
Instead of Heroes bold—to lead
A nasty filthy grunting Breed!
Yet, who can tell, but that, by chance,
He and his Swine may conquer France!

→

We're only Swine!—What humble pride!
That nobles design us on to ride!
Yea Monarchs mount our bristly back,
And make each joint and sinew crack!
We groan beneath the ponderous weight,
Of all the creatures of the State!
Placemen and Pensioners (beside
An innocent, caterpillar tribe)
In greedy swarms upon us ride!

The Mighty who in splendour shine,
May thank their Stars that there are Swine;
For, were we all of noble birth,
Where would we be Swine to root the earth,
To sweat and toil for their support,
Or, when they please, to be their sport?

Then hold not Swine in such disdain,
Since 'tis by them you have your gain;
But learn to treat them with respect,
Lest they should grunt at your neglect:
For, should they be provok'd!—What then?
The Swine would rise—and rise to MEN!

Norton, May

The Ox Over Driven;
an Original Fable

Twas on a Smithfield Market-day,
Two Drovers, full of ale and play,
An Ox were driving out to graze;
Thro' various streets, thro' various ways,
Gentle and harmless on he went,
No harm he thought — no mischief he meant,
Till beat and prick'd and goaded sore,
The beast began to run and roar;
In every street where he appear'd,
The cry, 'Mad Ox, Mad Ox' was heard,
Men, Women, Boys and Bawling throngs,
Pursued the fugitive along;
This way and that he took his course,
And all submitted to his force,
Stalls, China, everything came down,
And terror ran thro' half the town;
Still roaring, foaming, running, kicking,
The Drovers still behind him pricking: —
When, suddenly, he turned around,
And hurl'd both Drovers from the ground,
A lost in air they sprawled amain,
Their bones came rattling down again;
And as they pour'd their parting breath,
Just in the agonies of death,
They groaned out this — 'How just our fate!
'Though now repentance is too late!
'Had we drove mildly on we know,
'We ne'er had made the *Ox* our foe;
'But, from our cruelty, we find,
'We both are justly paid in kind'.

→

The fable told—the Moral's next,
At which some people may be vex'd;
But what care I for their vexation,
Themselves must make the application:
The Ox the PEOPLE plain discovers,
Suppose the MINISTRY the Drovers;
Who having gall'd and prick'd the nation,
Have found, at last, to their vexation,
That Britons may obey through love,
They may be led, but won't be drove.
—Then, let the *Drovers* of the State,
Beware the Smithfield Drovers fate,
And cease their galling, base oppression,
Ere they be brought to their confession!

By A Reformer of Sheffield

The Mad Man's Petition

Give me, ye Gods! A farm as snug
As woolen blanket to a bug;
I'll dance and sing, and rhyme and sleep,
To lowing cows and bleating sheep;
Carve Nancy's name on every tree,
But Nancy's false—as false as me!
A plague consume the filthy cot,
Perish the herds—the sheep may rot!

Give me a warehouse cramm'd with goods,
And filthy ships to plough the floods;
I'll strut and swear, and job and range,
The fiercest merchant upon 'Change;
—No, by my truth, I'll leave the Stocks,
To Bears and Bulls and waddling ducks.

How wretched is a bach'lor's life!
Give me, ye Gods, a pretty wife!
As Pallas wise, as Venus fair,
Gay as the light, as chaste as the air,
—No, now I think on't, wives have tongues,
And mine are weak, consumptive lungs.

Then grant me an enormous wig,
And fable coat, ten times too big:
With purple, pimpled face I'll shine
A worthy orthodox divine:
Six days and nights in riot spent,
Hallow the seventh and repent,
Then off again on Monday morn,
Nor rest still sabbath day return:
—No, my good Granmum used to say,
That there will come a Judgement Day!

→

Well then I'll be a soldier brave,
A Soldier's coat fits fool or knave;
With tongue of brass and heart of self-ware,
As thousands more beside myself are,
Like Hercules I'll mount a breach,
And butcher all within my reach:
'Stop', roars a bullet, 'Damn your eyes',
Cries Hercules—and falls—and dies!
A rout succeeds, a rout, a rout!
I cannot run—confound the gout!
Then give me, Jove, an hermit's cell,
Where I live like snail in shell,
And like another honest Ass,
Drink the clear spring and feed on grass;
From mourn to night, in my retreat,
I'll eat and bray, and bray and eat!

—No, who would be an Ass, that can
In any shape be—Man?

Give me a house in Grosvenor-square,
With forty thousand pounds a year;
An host of friends to wait my call,
Yet not a friend amongst them all!
But who would sigh for loss of friends,
A Star and Garter make amends;
Nicknames and fools—caps are ador'd,
Heav'ns! what a thing, to be a LORD!
Then in a chariot to be whirl'd,
And kick a dust up in the world!
—Hold!—Carriages are apt to break,
And mine's a very brittle neck;
'Tis fun to thunder up and down,
But not to fall and crack one's crown;
Sweet is the noise of rattling stones,
But curse the crash of rattling bones!

What shall I ask for next, ye Gods!
Of all this world's evens, or its odds,
Alike to me is odd or even,
There's no such thing on Earth, as Heav'n!
I bow to content to your decrees—
Give me, O give me—what you please!

By J. M. G.
Sheffield, Aug 12 1793

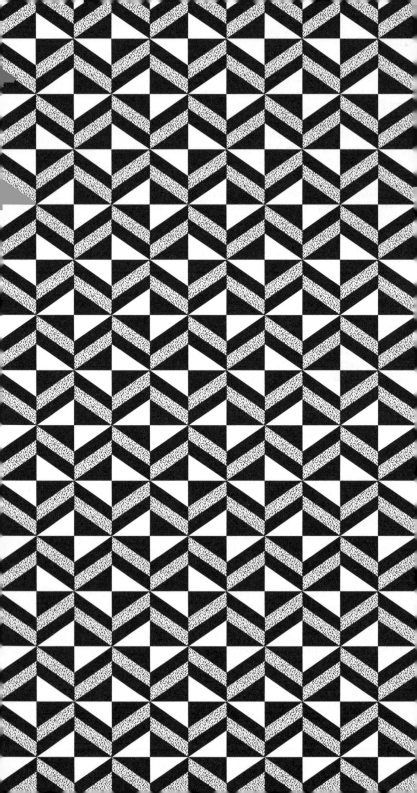

The Slave Trade

On reading the late Debate in the House of Lords upon the Bishop of Rochester's Motion respecting THE SLAVE TRADE.

Go, soft Humanity, thou whimpering fool!
Go, go, to CLARENCE's and THURLOW's school;
They'll teach thine eyes like red hot balls to burn,
Thy face to flint, thine heart to marble turn;
And pert Lord ABINGDON, so kind and civil,
Will kick — aye kick thee to the very Devil.
Come, dry those Tears for fable Slaves that flow,
Think'st thou that Negro-flesh can feel a blow?
Think'st thou the Almighty ever cramm'd a soul,
O horrible! — in such a dead *black* hole?
No, no, they're Asses, downright Brutes, I swear,
Mind that — and contradict me, if you dare.
Know that their Sweat, their blood, their Groans, their Sighs,
The Tears of *fifteen million* pairs of Eyes,
These with God's gracious blessing yield us clear,
Think *Providence*! *Four million pounds* a year!

By Paul Positive
Sheffield, March 19 1794

Commentaries

A Loyal Song
Sheffield Register No 303
23 March 1793

Songs have two parts: the air (tune) and the lyric. The tune to which words were set could be a political gesture, often counterpointing the sentiments of the words themselves. Here the tune is 'Derry Down', with at least 21 distinct iterations recorded as appearing between 1750–1800. 'Derry Down' later became inextricably tied to the plight of America during the Revolutionary Wars after it was employed in *The Gentleman's Magazine* (1766) to criticise the British government's mistreatment of American colonists. When British forces surrendered at Yorktown in 1781 they did so to this tune, arranged then in its most common late 18th-century formulation: 'The World Turned Upside Down'. After 1781 'Derry Down' retained an association with resistance to the British government in a more general sense.

These connotations persist in 'A Loyal Song', printed in the *Sheffield Register* No 303 on 23 March 1793 in response to Britain's involvement in the ongoing French Revolutionary Wars. The poem's address to the 'Old Tars of Old England' is an ironic one, deliberately inverting the poem's titular identification as a 'Loyal Song' and aligning itself with the sentiments typically associated with its chosen tune.

The poem's pose is deceptively complex; playfully appropriating the pro-war rhetoric of the social superiors it is addressing in order to render their enthusiasm absurd through bathos and hyperbole. Whilst the opening lines implore readers to 'cheer up', the reasons given encourage precisely the opposite response. In each of the quatrains to follow the song delivers a further caution against adventures in foreign war, packaging criticism as a satirical endorsement. It is alleged that the war will be paid for by unaffordable taxation on struggling British citizens with no stock in this conflict, the French have no inclination to fight Britain, and European commentators consider further conflict unnecessary. Nevertheless, Britain is going to war and as a 'Loyal Song' this poem must praise the fact, no matter how absurd its justifications.

The final stanza renders the poem's subtext overt as it identifies commercial gain as Parliament's true reason for waging an unnecessary war. It is in the final couplet that this song hits its target, capturing a cry of moral outrage that would come to characterise most of the poems printed in the *Register* throughout 1793. For the author of these lines the war itself is less offensive than the assumption that British citizens will accept their government's decisions without debate and discussion, encouraged instead to support the traditional powers that be, come what may:

> Our Rulers don't wish us to think of such things,
> Tis enough if we fight for CHURCH, LORDS and KINGS.

–

To read and listen to different iterations of 'Derry Down' and other songs of the American Revolution, visit *Digital History* (ed. By S. Mintz and S. McNeil, 2016): www.digitalhistory.uh.edu.

On the Effects of Gold
Sheffield Register No 304
29 March 1793

Although this is the only poem attributed to C. B. in the *Sheffield Register* in 1793, it picks up on a theme that recurs throughout these papers and adopts a very familiar pose, apparently praising that which it actually seeks to criticise. The poem chimes well with one of Joseph Gales' chief anxieties: that either a lack or excess of monetary capital might affect an individual's legal rights and political representation. The greatest challenge to social equality is identified throughout the *Register* as being man's commitment to personal capital gain over the well-being of the wider community. This poem apparently praises that reality, recalling the strategy of 'A Loyal Song' (printed just a week earlier) as it invites incredulity from its readers, covertly lampooning the statements it appears to endorse.

The poem presents its addressee with a series of complicated scenarios before revealing that each can easily be resolved with gold, imagined here as a 'magic wand'. Pulling no punches, the poem associates this phenomenon with political corruption, hinting that gold greases the wheels of government at every conceivable level, in 'country and senate and city'.

This theme continues into the second quatrain, addressing MPs looking for the support of voters. It suggests that prospective MPs need only take from their chest of riches (their 'coffer') some of their most valuable possessions (their 'pelf'), and upon seeing such treasure the wretched voter 'having nothing to offer, will frugally sell [them] himself'. It imagines the vote, the keystone of democracy, as a currency that can be bought and sold by the rich and the desperate: by far the poem's most scurrilous move. Taking an allegorical turn, the poem imagines gold not only as a hunter's weapon, employed for shooting fowl and catching fish, but as a device which can even prompt these animals to offer themselves up as an attractive meal 'ready drest in your dish'. The second half of the poem lists others who can be manipulated by gold. Therefore, the poem concludes, surely the pursuit of anything but capital gain is a waste of time.

The true purpose of this ironic resolution is to point a finger at those who are not only implicated in this corrupting obsession with money but responsible for its centrality to all social discourse: 'Priests, Ladies, Lawyers and Kings'. A final irony of the poem is the paradox that whilst gold will forever prevent the possibility of that equality later imagined by Gales in his final editorial *(see Appendix 5)* it also proves here to be society's greatest leveller. The poem may close with its gaze rested on 'Lawyers and Kings', but in the lines leading to this moment its interest in gold is one seen to be shared by 'wretches' at every rung on the social ladder.

The Bull
Sheffield Register No 306
12 April 1793

Though this is the first to explicitly address itself to John Bull he is a character named and referred to with discernible regularity throughout the poems of the *Sheffield Register*. He was last seen, for instance, in 'A Loyal Song', printed just two weeks earlier.

A common political caricature of the early 18th century, John Bull does not stand for court or crown but instead the good (and usually provincial) British citizen. In 'The Bull', written in Sheffield in 1793, we find a John Bull subjugated by the very people running the nation. As hinted in the two poems to precede this one, those at the top benefit from the subjugation of those at the bottom; on this occasion, the mighty John Bull.

The opening lines gloriously celebrate the strong, brave and majestic figure of John Bull ('awful' here employed in its typical 18th-century sense as meaning 'awe-inspiring'). Bull arrives in this poem like a cross between Homer's Zeus and Milton's Satan, with a 'voice of thunder', a 'lightning eye' and 'fire in every vein'. As a result of this it comes as quite a shock when the poem reveals that 'so much strength' is matched by 'so much weakness', for this majestic and awesome figure is prepared to bow passively when led by this 'string'.

The bull is described as a beast and, although he is majestic (described as both a 'monarch' and a 'king'), he is also 'savage'. His kingly attributes are derived from nature rather than the divine right that installs those monarchs at the head of state, making him their raw and unrefined counterpart. That the bull remains very much an animal throughout the poem adds weight to the next section, which sees this proud creature led to slaughter.

When the bull finds himself confronted with the pestilence and slaughter his courage awakens and he is compelled to make a sudden stand. His efforts are met with force, and in moments he is tied to a stake, a 'moaning victim left to wait in agonizing pangs, his lingering fate'. When you reflect that John Bull is no single man but a metonym for the honest men and women of rural Britain, this harrowing image of his torture at the hands of those at the very head of state is rendered all the more shocking.

Until this point the poem has observed events, recording the fate of the bull and encouraging readers to map his fate onto analogous trials faced in recent months by the population of Great Britain. Here, we see a faint shift, anchored by the suddenly modal word 'should':

> O! In that moment dart through frame,
> Should sudden fury touch his powers of flame.

From then on the poem no longer delivers a commentary but a hypothesis, imagining the bull's riotous but righteous revolt. In a single move he uproots the post to which he's tied and brings down the roof. Crucially, the roof is unsupported, symbolic of a regime which this poet finds illegitimate and with neither public nor divine backing. When it topples, so too does 'death and destruction, terror and dismay'.

'Terror' is burdened with some very specific connotations here, evoking the recent French Revolution and the tyrannical regime that led to it. This poem is imagining a British equivalent to France's Revolutionary wars, in which John Bull and the men and women he represents stand up to an equally tyrannous monarch; a seditious sentiment which has only the poem's necessary lurch into speculative territory for protection.

The final lines explicitly evoke James Thomson's lyrics to the 1740 song 'Rule, Britannia'. That song, an unapologetic work of staggering patriotism and uncomfortable British exceptionalism featured the unforgettable refrain:

> Rule Britannia, Britannia rule the waves;
> Britons never will be slaves.

This sentiment is amplified via the power of the 'People's Voice'; a voice that will not only resist the tyranny of foreign monarchs but also its own; a voice not satisfied with its own freedom, but proud to pursue the cause of freedom for the entire universe:

> For Freedom all the Nations look to thee;
> Britannia speaks and bid the Universe be free.

For more information on the character of John Bull we recommend Tamara Hunt's *Defining John Bull: Political Caricature and National Identity in Late Georgian England* (Routledge, 2003).

No Libel to Think
Sheffield Register No 307
19 April 1793

This is the only poem in the *Sheffield Register* attributed to T. G. but its appearance in April 1793 proves timely and prophetic. Over the coming months Joseph Gales work on the paper and his involvement in Sheffield's 'Society for Constitutional Information' would be met with increasing scrutiny from the authorities. In June 1794 he would be named a fugitive accused of printing libellous material with the explicit intent of rousing public animosity against the government. Over the two years that followed Gales' successor, James Montgomery, would be twice imprisoned on dubious charges of distributing libellous materials and on each occasion his defence attorney raised the same questions as this poem: what exactly constitutes libel?

The *Oxford English Dictionary* reveals that in the 18th century the word libel referred to the 'spreading of defamation; to maliciously discredit by circulation of false statements.' Neither Montgomery nor Gales ever disputed this definition, but they each argued that it did not apply to the material that they printed. In Montgomery's second case he was imprisoned for reporting that the British Army had charged down protestors in Sheffield. That this happened was never in question, the state prosecution did not challenge that. Instead they argued that in writing and circulating the report in the *Sheffield Iris* Montgomery had deliberately and maliciously defamed His Majesty's Army. What constitutes 'libel' is far more subjective than the letter of the law would suggest, especially when the statements challenged concern opinions and not events.

'No Libel to Think' begins by adopting a pose reminiscent of those employed in both 'A Loyal Song' and 'On the Effects of Gold', enthusiastically presenting the view it actually opposes in such cheerfully hyperbolic terms that it is rendered absurd. The poem appears to happily accept that, in this state of oppression, to complain verbally would bring about a citizen's 'destruction'. Fortunately citizens at least retain the 'freedom to think'. The second stanza qualifies that it is not speaking that is prohibited, merely speaking *'all* we think'.

The turn in this poem comes sooner than in the 'Loyal Song' or 'Effects of Gold' as the third stanza acknowledges that any suggestion that a state in which these conditions are enforced is clearly not 'perfect and pure.' In fact, the danger implicit in having the 'freedom to think' is that citizens have the capacity to realise that their liberties are being infringed. The rhetorical question used as a refrain up until this point is then extended throughout the fourth and fifth stanzas as the poem explicitly names the problems that citizens can think on but never utter aloud. These issues are predominantly financial. The poem challenges the reader: should a man have to pay to marry his wife or bury his dead? How can such a man afford food and shelter when 'they stamp us, and tax us both living and dead'?

The answer, of course, is no: a man should not be forced to pay for the privilege of participating in these private rituals. However, having had the freedom to realise this and identify the need for resistance, how then can this poem's narrative voice justifiably continue in silence? If to utter his concerns is to commit libel, the freedom to think has brought him no other choice:

And yet at such hardship they wish us to wink;
But we cannot do this—while we've freedom to think.

As the poem concludes we see that the freedom to think can lead to only one logical conclusion: men have rights and those rights must be defended.

Lines
Sheffield Register No 312
24 May 1793

In 1793 Britain was at war with France. The Bastille had fallen in 1789 prompting revolutionary war out across France. In September 1792 France had been proclaimed a republic. Shortly afterwards, the French king Louis XVI was executed. In 1793 Britain's government collaborated with other European powers in order to fight the new French republic and to restore the French monarchy.

The briefest survey of the *Sheffield Register* during this period reveals that opinions on the French Revolution were divided. Gales and most of his contributors supported the abolition of absolute monarchy, reading the overthrowing of Louis XVI as a much overdue equivalent to England's Glorious Revolution or the more recent American Revolution. The Republic, after all, stood for liberty: the *Register's* most passionate cause. However, as events escalated there emerged a discernible anxiety in the *Register* about the Republic's methods (most notably the imprisonment and subsequent execution of Marie Antoinette).

Unsurprisingly, Britain's war with France became one of the most common topics for the poems printed in the *Register* in 1793–94. Again, the tone and position of these poems is wildly inconsistent. Some are deeply patriotic, focusing on the bravery of British soldiers abroad. Others are pessimistic, criticising the Prime Minister's decision to involve Britain in the conflict.

A poem printed in the nineteenth issue of the *Register*, ironically titled 'Patriotism' *(see Appendix 1)*, provoked a high number of complaints and retaliatory poems. The poem proved controversial for its depiction of these young men, cheering a false cause as they marched off to an unnecessary death. It concludes that:

> But soon I trust these noisy knaves
> Will be what Nature meant them — Slaves.

The poem was roundly criticised for its pejorative portrayal of working-class men (prompting a lengthy series of poems on the topic of Britain's 'swinish multitudes'), but specifically for its unsympathetic portrayal of British soldiers. Although readers (and contributing poets) were prepared for the rationale behind this war to be troubled, the soldiers themselves were beyond reproach. A month after 'Patriotism' was printed these 'Lines' appear, compensating for the offense caused by that earlier contribution by lamenting the loss of life incurred by war.

These 'Lines' are tentatively attributed to a young woman living in Sheffield who has read in the previous issue of the *Register* about the death of a group of British soldiers during a violent skirmish with the French. Upon reading of the bravery of these soldiers our narrator recalls the bravery of her lover, Willy, who is currently fighting in France. If it were 'the bravest soldiers' who fell she deduces that one of them must have been Willy, prompting her to imagine his unburied body, left to rot and mould in some forgotten corner of a foreign field. The lover's name recalls that of the Prime Minister, William Pitt, highlighting the distance between soldier and statesman.

The poem not only mourns Willy's loss of life but that the narrator is robbed of the opportunity to be involved in his burial. Repeatedly she imagines herself beside the body, able to close his eyes with her own fingers and clasp him to her breast. This dream fades away as she laments that she is actually 'so far away', begetting the ghoulish image of Willy's lifeless and unburied form. She prays for the opportunity (using the now antiquated term 'boon') to put him to rest, but knows this plea is made 'in vain'.

The final stanza sees our narrative voice describing the scene she wishes she could enact, but knows she never will:

> To see that youth, who once was brave!
> O'er his lov'd form to sit and weep;
> And bid in peace his spirit sleep.

—
For an accessible and readily available introduction to the French Revolution and Britain's involvement in the ensuing conflicts we recommend William Doyle's *The French Revolution* (Oxford University Press, 2001) and Paul Langford's *Eighteenth-Century Britain* (Oxford University Press, 2000).

The Statesman's Soliloquy
Sheffield Register No 313
31 May 1793

The satire of 'The Statesman's Soliloquy' rests on the character's ludicrous fears of the word 'reform', imagined here as a demonic and destructive power that has come to purge all traces of the existing democratic system. Libertior's joke is grounded in bathos. This is funny because reform is not an apocalyptic force but a civilized aspect of the political process. That said, the poem's ambitions are two-fold, simultaneously lampooning the statesman's fears of reform whilst reassuring the *Register's* readers that these fears are absurd and deserving of ridicule.

In framing the poem as a soliloquy (the act of speaking one's thought aloud, often seen in theatrical drama) Libertoir takes the tendency of previous *Register* poems to ironically adopt an opposing attitude to more overt extremes. In the opening lines we witness the Statesman's sheer panic upon hearing the forbidden word 'reform'. It is a torturous, tormenting force to be dreaded. However, though it is initially feared for the violence of its execution we soon see the true reason our Statesman flees from reform. He is afraid he would lose his pension and no longer be at liberty to partake in bribery and treachery. The juxtaposition of the Statesman's initial notion of reform as an almost cosmic force of destruction and the banality of its actual effects not only achieves bathos but also invite readers to scrutinise representations of reform that they might encounter elsewhere.

It is only in the final couplet that the poem's narrative voice speaks for itself, observing the Statesman as he hurries off to Stephen's Gate (in Westminster) and promising readers that despite the politician's ability to avert his fears this long, reform is still coming for him:

> —He ceas'd and hurrying to Stephen's Gate,
> Finds still new cause to curse his pending fate.

—

For a concise overview of significant campaigns for reform at the dawn of the 19th century and their impact on later Chartist movements we recommend Dorothy Thompson's *The Chartists: Popular Politics in the Industrial Revolution* (Aldershot, 1986) and Christopher Harvie and Henry Matthew's *Nineteenth-Century Britain* (2000).

The Observations of a Swine, on the Condition of his Fellow Creatures

Sheffield Register No 317 28 June 1793

As the introductory note printed above this poem makes clear, it is addressed to 'Patriotism' *(see Appendix 1)*, a poem printed a month earlier in the *Sheffield Register* 309. However each of these texts is in dialogue with a third text: Edmund Burke's *Reflections on the Revolution in France* (1790). Burke argues that it was the sharing of learning with the masses that brought about revolution:

> Learning paid back what it received to nobility and to priesthood, and paid it with usury, by enlarging their ideas and by furnishing their minds. Happy if they had all continued to know their indissoluble union and their proper place! Happy if learning, not debauched by ambition, had been satisfied to continue the instructor, and not aspired to be the master! Along with its natural protectors and guardians, learning will be cast into the mire and trodden down under the hoofs of a *swinish multitude* (Penguin edn., 1968, p. 22).

People, Burke argues, should stay in their proper place. The 'swinish multitude' soon became shorthand for any political philosophy defending and perpetuating rigid social hierarchy. Burke is arguing that those disenfranchised in society, the people with the least, deserve their subjugation.

The statement alone prompted a plethora of responses criticising Burke's logic. In 2008 Darren Howard collated many of these, which included Daniel Isaac Eaton's 'Hog's

Wash' (1794), Thomas Spenser's 'Pig's Meat: Or, Lessons from the Swinish Multitude' (1793) and James Parkinson's 'Address to the Hon. Edmund Burke from the Swinish Multitude' (1793). Two issues later the *Register* would go on to publish its own poetic response to Burke: Mr Cooper's 'Swinish Herd to Edmund Burke'.

'Observations' centres its attack on the employment of Burke's phrase to describe British soldiers as a 'swinish rabble' in No 309's poem 'Patriotism'. The sentiments are difficult to gauge given the penchant of most *Register* poems to adopt attitudes they oppose in order to present them as absurd ('A Loyal Song' remains the clearest example of this strategy). The poem gleefully asserts that young soldiers fighting in France do not understand why they are there and claims that they should not be taken seriously. A more generous reading would see this poem as hinting that if they understood the rationale for Britain's war they would not be as quick to cheer their nation's cause. However, reading it straight (as 'Observations' clearly does), the poem appears to suggest that the soldiers enlisted in the British army were born to die and shouldn't be permitted to do anything else. They should never, for instance, become involved in politics or ever cast a vote. This second reading situates 'Patriotism' far closer to Burke's *Reflections* and as a result 'Observations' reads as a vehement attack on both.

The opening line lifts directly from the final couplet of 'Patriotism', recasting it as a question rather than a conclusive statement: did nature mean us to be slaves? Adopting the literalised voice of Burke's allegorical swine the poem's first stanza contests the implications of this question. It refrains from making statements, instead inferring its conclusions through a series of rhetorical questions. First it implies that surely the 'swinish multitudes' retain some claim to 'common rights and common sense' (evoking another revolutionary tract of political philosophy: Thomas Payne's *Common Sense*, 1776).

Extending Burke's unfortunate metaphor to uncomfortable lengths 'Observations' imagines the swinish population bred purely to be consumed by their social masters:

> And when they've fattened to be taken
> And quarter'd into hams and bacon,
> To satiate those who think it fit,
> To eat the carcase bit by bit

The power of this image is derived from its use of an unstable allegory. It is never clear whether the poem is referring to the actual relation between man and pig or that which it is elsewhere used to represent; the relationship between rich and poor. The slippage here is useful, facilitating an image of the gentry feasting on the fatted carcasses of the peasantry that never actually needs committing to pen and ink.

There is a refrain used to introduce the following three stanzas which revives the *Register* tradition of cheerfully embracing an opposing view for the purposes of ridicule and satire. Here it is the phrase 'We're only Swine!' delivered before six or seven lines justifying why this can't be true. The second stanza stages reversal: if the King is sovereign over swine then what does that make him in turn?

'Observations' then derives a perverse comedy from again literalising Burke's image and applying it to the scenes described in 'Patriotism':

> We're only Swine!—think but what fun,
> To see a Pig strut with his gun!
> How fierce and terrible the fight,
> To march large herds of Swine to fight!

In the closing stanzas this poem does something unlike any of the preceding *Register* satires. It stops criticising the idea that the poor are swine and embraces it, rebranding Burke's insult as a source of pride and inspiration. There would be no society if it wasn't for the labouring classes:

> We groan beneath the ponderous weight,
> Of all the creatures of the state.

What is more, these multitudes are only swine in the allegorical sense. They are, of course, *literally* men and they demand the respect of other men like Burke, leaving him to ponder on how logical it really is to insult a large populace of strong, labouring men:

> But learn to treat them with respect,
> Lest they should grunt at your neglect:
> For, should they be provok'd!—what then?
> The Swine would rise—and rise to MEN!

–
To read more about the many reactions and responses to Edmund Burke's *Reflections on the Revolution in France* we recommend Darren Howard's 'Necessary Fictions: The 'Swinish Multitudes' and the Rights of Man' in *Studies in Romanticism*, vol 47, No 2 (2008).

The Ox Over Driven; an Original Fable

Sheffield Register No 321
26 July 1793

'The Ox Over Driven' presents the most explicit criticism of the British constitution printed in the *Sheffield Register* in 1793, actually referring to the government's oppressive regime in its closing couplet. Written by 'A Reformer of Sheffield', the poem sets out to change ministerial practice and ensure better treatment of the general population. It was sensible to avoid charges of treason and sedition by presenting this critique as a fable (although this was somewhat undermined by the key to the poem's allegory presented in the second stanza).

Typically understood as being fictional tales designed to impart a moral lesson, fables lend themselves very well to allegory. In this poem, which positions itself as an 'original fable', we find two drovers (dealers in cattle) leading an Ox through Smithfield market.

We are told that the Ox is 'gentle and harmless'. Unfortunately the drovers are 'full of ale and play' and drunkenly begin goading the Ox, beating and pricking him until he is sore. The Ox, who had previously no thoughts of causing harm, is provoked into a feral rage. At this point the poem recalls No 306's poem 'The Bull', in which John Bull means to submit passively to the King and government but is ultimately provoked into revolutionary action to defend his country from pestilence and ruin.

None of the witnesses present have any sympathy for the Ox. Instead he is described as being 'mad' and chased. As he smashes the market, appropriately taking out a china stall, the poem describes the 'terror [that] ran through half the town'. As seen elsewhere in this collection 'terror' had a very specific resonance in 1793, evoking the actions of the new French Republic during the revolutionary wars.

At this point the Ox turns on the drovers (who are still pricking him) and mauls them almost to death. As they take their dying breath the drovers have just enough time to lament that they had no need to make the Ox their enemy and have no one to blame for events but themselves:

> But, from our cruelty, we find,
> We both are justly paid in kind.

In the second stanza this poem goes to great pains to disabuse readers of any notion that this poem might actually be about the mistreatment of livestock at Smithfield market. 'The fable told', it explains, 'the Moral's next'. The Ox in the poem is revealed to represent 'the people' and the Drovers 'the Ministry', or more generally, the government. If the Ministry continues galling and pricking the people, the poem warns, it will share the fate of the Smithfield Drovers. Remarkably the poem does not strike a hypothetical stance; it does not prophesise a dystopian future as seen in previous poems. 'The Ox Over Driven' is rooted firmly in the present tense, referring to the current state of affairs:

> And cease their galling, base oppression,
> Ere they be brought to their confession!

The Mad Man's Petition
Sheffield Register No 325
25 August 1793

Signed J. M. G., this poem was written by James Montgomery less than a year before he became editor of the *Register's* successor, the *Sheffield Iris.* In a letter written to Joseph Aston (later published posthumously in John Holland and James Everett's composite biography *Memoirs of the Life and Writing of James Montgomery,* 1855), Montgomery helpfully signs off by disclosing a list of pseudonyms that he and Aston published under in the *Register:*

> Paul Positive, Esq., Marcellus Moonshine, J. M. G., Plato, and 40,000 other idle fellows send their best respects to you and Peter Dubious.

The poem follows on nicely from No 313's 'The Statesman's Soliloquy' which similarly committed to presenting a monologue delivered in the voice of a fully formed fictional character. Here, Montgomery adopts the voice of a 'mad man' petitioning the gods. The use of the word 'petition' here is significant for its double meaning, as both an official request (as made to the government by reformers) and, in more antiquated usages, as a prayer or supplication. Montgomery's narrator is petitioning his gods to help find him a role in society, prompting a survey of positions perceived as being available to men at the end of the eighteenth century. In delivering this survey Montgomery also successfully touches upon the themes and concerns of many of the preceding poems, referring to monetary corruption, the violent and unnecessary war with France and the perverse and terrible gap between rich and poor.

Our narrator's first impulse is to find a life in the country, immediately evoking the rustic and dream-like vision of rural living typified by pastoral poetry. The pastoral was a popular mode with roots that could be traced back to the poetry and drama of the ancient world. The pastoral, however, deals in idealised representations of rural life with only a cursory engagement with actual conditions at the time of composition. As a result, the narrator's dream fades away before him as he admits that his pastoral sweetheart, Nancy, exists only in the mind's eye.

Next he imagines himself as a merchant before soon realising that the typical vision of the trader is yet another fantasy. Merchants might walk and talk a certain way, they can 'strut and swear, and job and range', but our narrator suspects this is just a performance. He is looking for a role where he can be authentic. Deciding that he will never be as happy as a bachelor he pauses briefly to imagine what it would be like to have a 'pretty wife', before again struggling to reconcile his ideals (a wife as fair as the Roman God Venus) with the reality of a wife who might talk and nag him all the time, straining his already weak respiratory system with stress.

Instead he then contemplates a life dedicated to religious worship. Unfortunately, in the poem's most topical allusion, he reflects on the disparity between his notion of a pious Christian and the recent behaviour of London's so-called 'Gordon Rioters' who, in the name of Protestantism, offered violent civil disturbance in the 1780s in support of anti-Catholic legislation. Perhaps, the narrator reflects, a military life awaits. He imagines himself storming the enemy like Hercules before noting once more that the reality would fail to live up to this fantasy. In actuality he has too much gout to take on any foe and recognizes that he would most likely die if faced with actual conflict. He briefly considers life as a hermit, eating and braying like an ass, but although this notion raises the least problems he concludes that he could never commit to such a lifestyle, for 'who would be an ass, that can be a man'.

Finally it seems that life as a London Lord with forty odd thousand pounds a year might be most appropriate. Then he could do whatever he pleased and never have to confront the disjunction between ideals and reality. With that amount of capital he could surely be his true self. Unfortunately, though he might be true to himself he has no assurances that 'friends' will be true to him. Attracted to his wealth he can no longer be sure that the affections of those around him are genuine, fearing instead that they represent little more than scheming and sycophancy.

As the poem draws to a close the so-called 'mad-man' determines that his pursuit is forlorn. Ideals and authenticity will always remain unachievable, for 'There's no such thing on Earth as Heav'n'.

—
For an accessible and readily available account of the Gordon Riots and their impact on reform efforts towards the end of the 18th century we recommend Paul Langford's *Eighteenth-Century Britain* (Oxford University Press, 2000).

The Slave Trade
Sheffield Register No 355
15 March 1794

Throughout the second half of the 1700s the gradual movement toward the abolition of slavery in Britain gained considerable momentum. The impulse to end the trade of human beings was the logical consequence of the discourse of rights which we have seen come to characterise the *Sheffield Register* poems of 1793–94. The recent events of both the American and French Revolutions had forcefully raised serious questions about fundamental constitutional norms. As more and more people concluded that all men had the right to be free the ethics and implications of the slave trade were met with new levels of scrutiny.

The *Register's* poem, 'The Slave Trade', is attributed to Paul Positive, a name later revealed in a letter to John Ashton as a pseudonym for James Montgomery. The cause of abolition would characterise much of Montgomery's later career. In 'The Slave Trade' Montgomery takes the most common trait of the *Register* poems, appropriating the arguments perpetuated by its opponents and expressing them with a hyperbolic enthusiasm that deliberately foregrounds their logical inconsistencies to ultimately render them absurd. Employing this technique in reference to the slave trade makes this simultaneously both one of the *Register's* most uncomfortable poems and one of its most effective.

Taking as its inspiration a parliamentary address delivered by Samuel Horsey, the Bishop of Rochester, which campaigned for a bill prohibiting Britain's involvement in the trading of slaves on the east coast of Africa, 'The Slave Trade' finds itself embroiled in the varying parliamentary positions touted at the time of print. The poem begins by apostrophising Humanity, addressed here as a 'whimpering fool'. Humanity is advised, ironically, to subscribe to 'Clarence and Thurlow's school' where it will learn to be unfeeling and impenetrable. This is not a literal school but rather a school of thought perpetuated by two of Britain's most prominent advocates of slavery at this time: William, Duke of Clarence and St Andrews (later King William IV) and Baron Edward Thurlow, the English Lord Chancellor.

The inference here is that to endorse slavery is to corrupt the soul, learning to feel hate rather than compassion if indeed you were to feel anything at all. The 'kind and civil' Lord Abingdon here is Bertie Willoughby, a figure remembered in the *Oxford Dictionary of National Biography* as a political writer who had supported the plight of the American colonists but opposed the new Republic of France. In Montgomery's poem, after Humanity has been thoroughly jaded by Clarence and Thurlow, Abingdon will be in position to kick it straight to hell.

The following lines mimic the various justifications for the persistence of slavery, sending up disturbing notions that slaves have no souls and therefore cannot feel pain. Recalling the moral outrage of earlier poems in this collection, particularly in 'On the Effects of Gold' and 'The Statesman's Soliloquy', Montgomery locates what he asserts to be the true resistance to abolition. It is not the absurd notion that all slaves are 'asses' and 'brutes' but the calculation made by men like Clarence and Thurlow that the 'tears of fifteen million pairs of eyes' are worth less than the 'four million pounds a year' earnt by Britain through the trade of slaves.

Thirty years before his death he observed that what might become of his name and writings in the next age was not for him to anticipate, and that he had honestly endeavoured to serve his own generation and, on the whole, had been careful to leave nothing behind him to make the world worse for his having existed in it. Montgomery not only showed by word and deed how life ought to be lived, but also transmitted a notable example of self-help and perseverance.

W. Odom, *Two Sheffield Poets: James Montgomery and Ebenezer Elliot*, (1929) p. 62.

For those who know where to look, the streets of Sheffield are paved with the story of James Montgomery (1771–1854). He is the namesake of the Montgomery Theatre, of Montgomery Road and of the one-time Montgomery Tavern. He is memorialised as a champion of causes. He was a vocal campaigner against slavery and religious intolerance, he was a supporter of universal access to education and political representation. On his death local government organised a city-wide funeral in his honour and the people of Sheffield raised funds for a life-size bronze statue. Half a century earlier the same local government had branded him a dangerous radical and he was twice imprisoned on charges of sedition and treason. In 1795 Montgomery was hauled in front of a jury in Doncaster for printing a poem in support of the French, Britain's enemies at the time. Montgomery's lawyer proved that not only did Montgomery have no knowledge of the poem in question, but that it had actually been written ten years previously. The poem had been addressed not to the current war with France but the events of the French Revolution. It was a compelling defence, documented and corroborated by numerous sources. Remarkably, Montgomery was still found guilty and sent to a prison in York. During his time in prison Montgomery produced a short volume of poetry titled *Prison Amusements,* capitalising on his incarceration to address a recurrent theme: every man's entitlement to freedom.

Within 18 months of his release he would find himself back in prison, this time for reporting that British soldiers had charged down a group of unarmed protesters in Sheffield. On the eve of this trial Montgomery wrote to his close friend, local author John Aston, lamenting that it didn't matter how strong a defence he presented, 'the prosecution is levelled against the *Iris;* they are determined to crush it' *['Letter to Joseph Aston', Sheffield Archives: SLPS/37 (1) 4 (B)].*

The *Register* and the *Iris*

The *Iris* mentioned above is the *Sheffield Iris*: the newspaper that Montgomery edited from 1794–1825 and the sequel to the city's most controversial paper, the *Sheffield Register*. It is amongst the pages of this paper, edited by Joseph Gales (1760–1741), that the story of this collection takes place. Montgomery at this point was not yet the man who would one day be memorialised in bronze beside Sheffield Cathedral. Nor was he the newspaper editor who would soon find himself stood before a jury in Doncaster. The Montgomery of this volume is the teenager who Joseph Gales took a punt on, hiring him as a jobbing-apprentice with no previous journalistic experience before quickly promoting him to editorial assistant.

At the time, young Montgomery was a teenage runaway. He had been born in Ayrshire, South-West Scotland, but upon discovering that his parents planned to become Unitarian missionaries and move abroad he fled to England. He was aiming for London where he aspired to make his name as a poet. Instead, he wound up in Rotherham. It was there that he applied to an advert in the local paper to work for Gales at the *Sheffield Register*.

The *Sheffield Register* had been founded by Gales with the explicit intention of not only keeping Sheffield citizens up to date with the latest news but also of championing the causes of freedom, liberty and reform. This second ambition would later be named as the paper's overarching *raison d'être* in the *Register's* last ever issue, which saw Gales commenting that:

> It will always be my pride that I have printed an impartial and truly independent newspaper, and that I have done my endeavours, humble and limited as they have been, to rescue my Countrymen from the darkness of ignorance and to awaken them to a sense of their

privileges as human beings, and, as such, of their importance in the grand scale of creation.

In a sequence of events foreshadowing the charges later levelled against Montgomery, the *Register* came to an abrupt close in June 1794. For his work on this paper and his role in founding Sheffield's controversial 'Society for Constitutional Information', Gales was forced to flee British shores as a felon charged with 'conspiracy against the government'. As an aspiring journalist, a close friend of Gales and a supporter of the *Register's* politics, Montgomery worked fast and hard to rally funds and support for a new paper, the *Sheffield Iris.* This new paper positioned itself as an explicit continuation of the *Register's* ethos and vision. Whilst Sheffield's rival Tory paper loudly celebrated Gales' disappearance from Sheffield, relieved that their city was no longer threatened by the opinions of a dangerous radical, Montgomery's *Iris* proudly acknowledged the personal and professional sacrifices he had made to protect the rights of his city's citizens.

The poems in this collection were all printed during the final year of the *Sheffield Register* (1793–94). This year saw the paper at its most radical, articulating its outrage at the government's management of the nation. Doing so in stirring prose and verse, it began to draw fire from the city's conservative and reactionary quarters. The *Sheffield Courant* (a rival paper) claimed that Gales was overstepping the mark, deliberately fueling dissent and dissatisfaction when he should have been providing a neutral commentary on local events. The Curate of Dronfield named Gales as a dangerous and irresponsible radical in a sermon which went on to be widely reported in the city's press. As Gales' 'Society for Constitutional Information' grew in both numbers and influence so too did the suspicions with which it was regarded by local authorities.

The poems printed this year show Gales' project at its most distilled, fearlessly shrugging off the ambiguity and allegory of the *Register's* earlier poems to reveal a series of carefully targeted and high-powered attacks.

Poetry Corner

Each issue of the *Register* was divided into five columns across four pages. Peppered with adverts throughout, the *Register* opened with a page of national (and often international) news, followed by a page of aggregated London news. Page three was dedicated to local news and page four was for letters, essays and addresses. It was on the fourth page of these papers that Gales introduced a feature that would be continued in Montgomery's *Iris;* a feature referred to affectionately in reader's letters as 'Poetry Corner'.

Known in the *Register* as the 'Repository of Genius' and the *Iris* as the 'Bower of Muses', this space saw the weekly publication of both locally produced poetry and works collected from elsewhere. The poems, which often write back to one another, demonstrate on the part of Gales and Montgomery an attempt to document and promote a network of poets across Yorkshire. Additionally, as this collection emphasises, 'Poetry Corner' also represented a deliberate attempt to build a coherent and effective platform for local protest at a time of profound anxiety and scepticism about top-down decisions made by a monarchy and government situated 170 miles south of Sheffield.

'Poetry Corner' showcased poetry both produced in Sheffield and from elsewhere. Some poems were lifted from other provincial newspapers printed in Newcastle, Manchester, Birmingham and Wakefield. Others were taken from the London press or even, in some instances, papers in America. In 1794, conventions of documenting where poems had come from or who had written them were inconsistent. Sometimes poems were introduced with an attribution, naming the paper in which they had first appeared. On other occasions the poems were simply presented in isolation. If poems had been sent in by the paper's readers they usually ended with a parenthetical note stating where the poem had been composed and on what day. It was very rare for these poems to appear with the author's name attached. Some were simply printed anonymously, likely due to their provocative content. Many were published under pseudonyms, most of which were only ever used once. Today's newspaper is built on the assumption of its redundancy tomorrow. As a result, the very medium in which these protest poems first appeared preserves their intended anonymity well into posterity. We may never know who or where some of the poems came from because we were never supposed to know.

Literary criticism

The poetry in this volume was written at the start of what is called the Romantic Period. It is a common but contested literary term. There are no exact dates, but as a rule-of-thumb it can be helpful to think of the Romantic Period as being roughly 1790–1840. Possible starting points include Robert Burns's 1786 volume of *Poems,* the storming of the Parisian Bastille in 1789, or even William Wordsworth and Samuel Taylor Coleridge's volume of poems called *Lyrical Ballads* (1798). Possible end dates might be the passing of the First Reform Act in 1832, the succession of Queen Victoria to the throne in 1837 or even the death of William Wordsworth in 1850. The poems in this volume challenge our assumptions about what constitutes the period because they do not fit easily into conventional academic assumptions about Romantic verse.

On the one hand, many of the poems clearly look backwards through literary history to a tradition of satire we associate with the early 1700s. Then, writers such as Alexander Pope, Jonathan Swift and John Gay satirised contemporary literary standards and combined that with deeply barbed observations about the government of the day and the corruption they perceived in society. Poems such as Pope's *The Rape of the Lock* (1712–17), plays such as John Gay's *The Beggar's Opera* (1728) and novels such as Jonathan Swift's *Gulliver's Travels* (1726) lie behind the satirical and often angry form, tone and content of poems in this volume. Such satirical material circulated throughout the century and there is no doubt that it came to form a canon of influential reading that influenced the readers of the *Register*.

If the poetry in the *Register* looks backwards in terms of its satirical and formal influences, it also reflects new forms of expression that we associate more with the Romantic literature of the 1790s. We find a firm expression of a singular sentimental voice in 'Lines' or 'The Mad Man's Petition' that would not look out of place in a collection such as *Lyrical Ballads*. 'No Libel to Think' borrows from the rhetoric of both the French and American revolutions, invoking ideas of freedom, liberty and equality that would be recognised by authors such as Robert Burns, Lord Byron, Mary Shelley or the young Wordsworth and Coleridge. 'The Slave Trade' voices emancipatory concerns that were to echo through British literature until the middle of the nineteenth century. Particularly in terms of voice and theme, then, these poems anticipate the next fifty years of Romantic poetry.

Thus the poems in this volume look both backwards and forwards in their concerns. In their demotic origin and popular dissemination they reflect, more accurately than perhaps current literary criticism allows, the emergence of the self-reflective and politically-engaged literary sensibility that we call 'Romantic Literature'. One final and important way in which we can read these poems is as a series of fragments (the literary fragment is a key Romantic idea – Coleridge's *Kubla Khan* (1816) is perhaps the most famous example). Each poem as it appears weekly in 'Poetry Corner' contributes to the whole: what Gales and Montgomery called the 'Repository of Genius' or the 'Bower of Muses'. No poem is itself a complete statement of the newspaper's ethos; no single poem expresses what the readership thinks or feels. Rather, each is a fragment of a wider whole: the literary sensibility of Sheffield.

Thematic approaches

As the *Register* explicitly acknowledges time and again, Gales was editing the paper in the shadow of the still recent French Revolution (1787) and amidst the social, political and cultural aftermath of Thomas Paine's *Rights of Man* (1791). Perhaps unsurprisingly then, the poems of the *Register* and the *Iris* are best unified by just such a central preoccupation: what are the fundamental rights and entitlements of all men? It is in forcefully answering this question that the most common themes of the collection come into focus. These poems assert time and again that all men should be free. Most of these poems can be seen to trace the various connotations and manifestations of that freedom. They discuss such issues as: parity in political representation, universal access to education, racial and religious equality, the abolition of slavery and the need for worker's rights.

Freedom from captivity

The most obvious short-hand for the infringement of civil liberties manifests itself in the paper's regular allusions (and direct references to) slavery. The paper witnesses the abolition of slavery in France in 1794 whilst vocally campaigning for abolition across the British Empire, a goal that would not be achieved until 1833. For the *Register,* slavery is the ultimate violation of man's rights and though it does endorse the freeing of actual slaves the topic is most often raised as a hyperbolic analogy for the mistreatment of British citizens under the government of William Pitt. Similarly, these poems often focus on instances of individuals being held captive against their will as an overt symbol of inhumane treatment, again prompting readers to reflect on any similarities between the treatment of these individuals and their own treatment as British subjects.

Freedom of speech

By far the most common preoccupation of these poems is the extent to which freedom extends to a subject's utterances and written expressions. A great deal of ink is spilt highlighting instances in which legitimate commentary on the policies and principles of crown and court are categorised as libel and met with punitive action. In response to these accusations of libel and sedition, these poems regularly assert that a truly democratic state relies on its citizens having the right to question and criticise its management. Indeed, above all else the freedom of the press is regularly identified within the *Register* as the last precaution against tyranny.

Freedom from political oppression

A key anxiety of the paper which becomes more apparent as it marches towards its final number is that the interests and welfare of Sheffield (and the North of England more generally) are not adequately represented by the government in Westminster. Preempting the Chartist movements of the midnineteenth century by some decades, the paper regularly published poems campaigning for political reforms that favour the rights and representation of a greater number of citizens from across Britain. These sentiments overlap with those of Joseph Gales' Sheffield-based 'Society for Constitutional Information'.

Freedom from economic constraints

It is a common occurrence for *Register* poems to apostrophise money, contemplating its power to both create and corrupt. The paper champions political representation for all British citizens, regardless of social standing and monetary income. The poems within the paper regularly suggest that those who have money and power are unlikely to share it for fear that it might compromise their hereditary positioning at the top of society. In his final editorial for the *Register* Gales acknowledged that he considered himself a poor man, along with most of his peers in Sheffield's 'Society for Constitutional Information' and the vast majority of his readers. He wrote that one of his most passionate ambitions was to demonstrate that all men, regardless of wealth, were entitled to respect and representation from their government.

This collection

With well over fifty poems printed in 'Poetry Corner' during the *Register's* final year in print we have had to be careful when choosing those that appear in this collection. We have chosen poems that are indicative of the style, tone and interests of the full corpus of *Register* poems. These papers represent an embarrassment of riches for not only literary scholars but also social and cultural historians and those interested in print culture and the evolution of the press. There are some remarkable poems that we have had to omit. Largely due to their appearance in a local and ephemeral publication, many of the poems are deeply committed to addressing specific issues emerging from day-to-day life in late eighteenth-century Sheffield. Whilst fascinating, the issues in such verse are deeply obscure when read today. However, even those poems locked into the granular detail of their own times are in tune with the broader themes of both the editorial strategy behind 'Poetry Corner' and the *Register* as a whole. It is these grander themes that the poems in this collection represent.

When a text is serialised, with a new instalment added at regular intervals for an indefinite period of time, interesting and peculiar things start to happen. If you have ever collected a magazine or followed a long running television program you will be familiar with these phenomena. You see the text in question strive to find its own identity, becoming more distinctive and coherent over time. You see the editorial team getting better at what they do, becoming more efficient and developing tropes, traits and short-hands unique to their publication. You see the form develop and evolve. Often claims are made retrospectively to a deliberate and overarching design as the publication works to flatten out its prior idiosyncrasies, fashioning its own history into something more consistent. These processes are magnified in the *Register's* 'Poetry Corner'. Reading them in order reveals the emergence of fixations amongst the paper's contributors: themes and topics that resurface time and again. Certain characters reappear, each time more clearly defined. Otherwise ordinary words and phrases become burdened with extra meaning. Some poems pick fights with past poems, whilst others pick up and carry torches.

For this reason, the poems in this collection have been arranged in the order that they were originally published. We recommend first reading them in this order. For example, passing references to John Bull become increasingly nuanced, culminating in 'The Bull': at once a detailed study of a British folk character and a rousing indictment of monarchy and government. Elsewhere, a throwaway reference to soldiers as 'swine' in the poem 'Patriotism' prompts two very different responses: 'Lines' offers a harrowing account of the human loss incurred by war whilst 'Observations of a Swine' critiques the earlier poem's troubling representation of working men.

These poems experiment with form. A recurring trait is that they adopt perspectives oppositional to their own, articulating them with such exaggerated enthusiasm and flagrant disregard for logic that they are rendered absurd. An obvious example of this would be the first poem, 'A Loyal Song'. By the time 'A Statesman's Soliloquy' is printed this satirical tendency has been fully integrated in the poem's form. Written as a dramatic monologue, the 'Soliloquy' not only allows the poet to parody political rhetoric, but the frame narrative also allows him a second voice with which he can criticise and condemn this language.

Adam James Smith and Hamish Mathison

Appendices

1.

Patriotism
Sheffield Register No 309
3 May 1793

Printed in response to Britain's involvement in the French Revolutionary Wars, this proved a controversial poem. It is explicitly criticised in 'The Observations of a Swine, on the Condition of his Fellow Countrymen' (No 317) and sits awkwardly alongside 'Lines' (No 312), each printed within a month of this poem's publication.

SHALL men who drudge from morn 'till night
Pretend to talk of wrong and right?
No, no, the sweat which toil produces,
Exhausts the intellectual juices,
And leaves the brain, that fine machine,
Unfit for aught, save what is mean.
Rouse then, Oh rouse! and crush these fellows,
Who are in Reason's cause so zealous,
Who dare to tell the *Swinish* rabble,
That all in Politics should dabble;
That every tattered greasy rouge
Who quash a pot, or wears a brogue,
Should vote for Senators, and be,
Like men of birth and fortune free.

But soon I trust these noisy knaves
Will be what Nature meant them—*Slaves*.

AN EPIGRAM
OF Generals don't tell me, of YORK, and such boys;
Nor of HOWE—tho' I mean not their laurels to taint;
The General I'm sure that will make the most noise,
If *the war should go on*—is—GENERAL COMPLAINT.

2. Letters
Sheffield Register No 332
11 October 1793

As was typical of serial print throughout the 1700s, the *Sheffield Register* was often embroiled in 'print wars' with other contemporaneous papers. Most often it found itself exchanging insults with its local Tory counterpart, the *Sheffield Courant.* The feud that prompted the letters below was particularly impassioned.

In September 1793 Reverend J. Russell, the curate of Dronfield, had publicly criticised Joseph Gales and implied his work on the *Register* was a form of treason against both his King and government. The sermon was celebrated in the *Courant* as part of a broader attack on the *Register,* led by the *Courant's* poet-in-residence.

Amidst the pages of the *Register* this series of events is reported as an insidious attack upon the freedom of the press. Gales uses his retaliation as an opportunity to assert that the press's capacity to offer commentary and criticism on the actions of government is the most significant indicator that a society retains a degree of liberty.

The letters transcribed here were alleged to have been submitted by the *Register's* readers. They show support for Gales in the face of the *Courant's* attacks.

2a. To the Printer of the *Sheffield Register*

SIR,

If you would give the following a place in your next paper, it might serve to contribute to the interest of an unfortunate fellow-creature, and promote the advantage of many, by rectoring a pious man to the exercise of that sacred function, to which he has always been so bright and ornament.

Yours, &c.
TOM TRIM

As it is certain, that the meanest even of DAGGER, BURKE'S multitude, will so far degrade himself, as to make any reply to the frantic effusions of a poor maniac, who calls himself J. RUSSELL; I feel myself constrained by the principle of humanity, seriously to request the parishioners of D——, who have long exercised their forbearance with the manners of their poor curate, to step forth in behalf of the friendless creature, and, in pity to his case, try the following method; which, by the blessing of God, may be effectual to his restoration, in as great a degree as so desperate a case can admit of.

Let his head be frequently shaved, and a large blister be applied to it. Continue him to a dark room. Let him be secured with a strong iron chain. Allow him plenty of clean straw; and, as his habit is exceedingly foul, copious evacuations should be effected. Let his diet be bread and water – The first symptoms of recovery will be a redness of the cheeks, with strong expressions of shame.

N. B. There is a little crooked-leg animal of cur breed, marked J. T. which continually disturbs the neighbourhood with his egregious howling. If the inhabitants were to lay out a few pence in whipcord, and employ some beggar's boy to whip the thing to his hole, it would be rendering a kindness to society.

2b.   To the Editor of the *Sheffield Register*

SIR,

It is with much concern that I see the abuse poured upon you from time to time through the medium from a certain apology for a weekly paper, entitled the *Courant*.

I think it my duty, as it is the duty of every honest lover of liberty, to support with all my power the independence of the *Register* – I have been astonished at the mad effusions of a few factious men, whose aim is to crush, not only the editor of the *Register,* but every friend of liberty and his country. One, in particular, under the title of J. RUSSELL, has uttered such infernal language against you, and the inhabitants of this town in general, as is unworthy of the notice of men of sound judgment, but the direct contrary: they merit our pity as men, but their principles meet with our contempt.

While RUSSELL and his associates, men of no consequence and no abilities, are talking of levelling and plundering I would recommend it to all your candid readers, to keep a strict eye over their hearts, and prove to the world, by their public and private conduct, that the opposers of reformation, are the only levellers and enemies to mankind.

Yours, &c.
PHILOM.

3.

James Montgomery; Complimentary Lines addressed to the *Sheffield Courant*

Sheffield Register No 332
11 October 1793

As detailed in Appendix 2, Reverend J. Russell (Curate of Dronfield) had criticised Joseph Gales and the *Sheffield Register* in a public sermon, claiming to have identified a treasonous project. The sermon was celebrated in the *Register's* rival paper, the *Sheffield Courant,* which also printed a panegyric poem championing Russell's claims. In the poem transcribed below James Montgomery responds in kind and in doing so invokes Alexander Pope's satirical method from earlier in the century. 'God save King Log' in the third line recalls the final line of the first book of Pope's poem *The Dunciad.* It was a renowned satire on bad poetry that had appeared in various revisions from the 1720s to the 1740s.

ONE day, a little coxcomb of a Frog,
Popped his grey nose from out a putrid bog,
'God save King Log,' he croak'd with all his might,
'And damn the Sun for standing in my light!'

So J.T.'s muse, a squint-ey'd wretch, who Fate
Ordain'd to send and swear in Billingsgate,
With yard-wide jaws, and longs as bagpipes strong,
To bellow 'Crabs and Lobsters,' all day long;
Assumes a courtly air, and strains to sing,
With laughing grimace, 'God save the King;'
Yet blasts the Freedom that bestow'd his Crown—
Freedom! the Guardian of the British Throne—
Freedom! by Slaves and Guilty Tyrants fear'd—
Freedom! by Men and virtuous King rever'd!

Thy strains, 'tis true, too stupid are too charm—
One comfort is, poor souls, they do no harm:
With slumbers soft they may relieve gout,
But cannot make the cripple dance about;
And tho' they cannot cure, yet may they steep
An aching head or broken heart in sleep:—
So a pert Cricket, perch'd upon the tongs,
Enchants the noisy kitchen with his songs,
Till romping Maids and Scullions romp no more,
But drop their dishclouts and their heads—to snore!

Still languish in thine obscurity,
And like thy worthy Brother-Spider be;
Who in the garret window weaves his snares,
To hamper flies as poachers hamper hares,
And as he riots on their blood alone,
Grumbles and growls like Mastiff o'er a bone.

Go, paltry reptile! Join thy Parson's rout,
And squirt with thy spleen and ink about;
Blot every honest name, till all are grown,
At least as black and baffled as your own;
Beat your swollen breasts with Envy's scorpions curst,
Rage on, brave pair, and welcome—till ye burst:
That Cause must needs be good, which meets with foes,
In TAYLOR's doggerel Rhymes and RUSSEL's ranting prose.

4.

James Montgomery; Address to the Sheffield Society for Constitutional Information

Sheffield Register No 334
25 October 1793

James Montgomery penned this public address in response to Reverend J. Russell's claims that Joseph Gales was involved in treasonous activity through both his work on the *Sheffield Register* and founding of the Sheffield Society for Constitutional Information. It was printed below a series of letters criticising Reverend Russell.

Fellow Citizens,

It is with trembling diffidence and conscious inability, I venture to address a Society so numerous and respectable. I have read with considerable attention the very ingenious reply to the calumnies of the Dronfield Curate, adopted and passed as the sense of the late meeting upon Crooksmoor. Had I possessed the commanding eloquence of a certain member of your Society, now absent, I should certainly have attended that meeting, and with all the united energy of diction and thought, supposed, not that address in particular (for upon the whole I very much approve of it) but every address, or serious answer, in any form, the contemptible croakings, there than by a few, short, pointed, laconic Resolutions!

[...] Nothing in Nature is, or can be produced perfect! Reason, the sun of the soul, the God within us, proceeds through various stages of idiotism in infancy, folly in childhood, giddiness in youth, 'til more and more matured by experience and reflection, at length it reaches the sublimity of sense! Creation itself, at the word of him who speaks WORLDS, rose gradually from the howling anarchy of Chaos, to the glorious perfection of the boundless Universe. He whose voice called the Universe into existence could have formed it in one moment, but he chose to complete his work in six days, and rested on the seventh, to teach man, whom he formed in his image, that every great, every arduous, every noble work must be the fruit, the reward, the crown, of persevering industry, and unwearied well-doing. Go on, therefore, friends of freedom, friends of mankind, go on. Tyranny, despotism and priestcraft must fall with a crash that will astonish the Universe. Therefore, INVINCIBLE, go on – PROSPER – and triumph.

5.
Joseph Gales;
The Editor's Address
Sheffield Register No 369
27 June 1794

Charged with 'conspiracy against the government' Joseph Gales was forced to stand down as editor of the *Sheffield Register,* bring the paper to an abrupt close. This address appeared in the *Register's* final instalment. Gales attempts to explain his actions, bid farewell to readers and formally draw the paper to close with a thematically consistent denouncement. Gales never did stand trial, instead fleeing Britain to ultimately start a new life in America.

After having lived ten years in Sheffield, and in habits of friendship with many respectable families in the town and neighbourhood, it is a painful task to bid them and my friends at large, a serious, and perhaps eternal, farewell. The disagreeable predicament in which I stand, from the suspension of the Habeas Corpus Act, precludes me the happiness of staying among you, my Friends, unless I would expose myself to the malice, enmity and power of an unjust aristocracy. It is, in these persecuting days, a sufficient crime to have printed a newspaper which has so boldly dared to doubt the infallibility of ministers, and to investigate the justice and policy of their Measures.

Could my imprisonment, or even death, sever the cause which I have espoused – the cause of peace, liberty, and justice, it would be cowardice to fly from it, but, convinced that ruining my family and distressing my friends, by risking either, would only gratify the ignorant and the malignant, I shall seek that livelihood in another state which I cannot peaceably obtain in this. To be accused is, now, to be guilty, and however conscious I may be of having neither done, said, or written, anything that mitigates against peace, order, or good government, yet, when I am told that witnesses are suborned to swear me guilty of treasonable and seditious practices, it becomes prudent to avoid such dark assassins, and leave to the informers and their employers the mortification of knowing, that however deep their villainy was planned, it has been unsuccessful.

My Friends, and many I gratefully acknowledge I have found, since my residence among you, will do justice to my actions and motives which impelled them – my Enemies will, as they have hitherto done, misconstrue my intentions, misrepresent my actions, and exaggerate my failings; but in the calm impartial moment of separation, I would tell them, with the firmness of my conscious Rectitude, that I dare any man, or set of men, to prove, even in a single instance, that I ever voluntarily injured an individual, or deviated from the strict line of moral rectitude which marks the honest Man and the useful Member of Society. I am accused of the heinous faults of having been a Member of the Constitutional Society – I was a Member of the Society of this Place, and shall never, I am persuaded, whatever may be the final result, regret it, knowing and believing that the real as well as ostensible object of this Society, was a rational and peaceable reform in the representation of the people in Parliament.

I know the Principles of the Society to be, generally speaking, those of peace and good-will to all mankind; and I never heard a sentiment, as coming from the Society, which was inimical to the purest System of Peace, Honesty, and good Order. The Secret Committee have imputed to the Society Intentions of which they had no Conception, and crimes which they abhor. The peaceable Manner in which they conducted their Meetings, their Modes of Proceeding, must evince the Injustice of the Constructions put upon their Intentions. None but venal, unjust, or prostigate Minds, can so far pervert the Principles of the Society, as to Impute to them a wish to overrun the present Form of Government. They published their intentions to Arm for Self-Defence, and the Internal Safety of the Kingdom; they avowed their motives, and they vindicated their Pretensions from a Clause in the Bill of Rights, that great Bulwark of British Freedom, which the suspension of the Habeas Corpus Act goes so nearly to sap. It was natural, that Poor Men, and of that Description are the major Part of the Society, should seek such Arms as their Circumstances would afford; And, even the Purchase of Pikes was more than their Finances would admit of, as appears by the very few manufactured.

IT has been insinuated, and, I believe, pretty generally believed, that I wrote the Letter which is referred to by the Secret Committee, concerning the Pikes, and given in the last *Register*. This Charge, in the most unequivocal manner, I DENY. I neither wrote, dictated, or was privy to it; nor, till Mr Hardy's apprehensions, had any Knowledge of it. As far as this stigma personally respects myself or Family, I am indifferent as to the Report, but I owe, to my Friends and the Public, the Duty of clearing myself from the Imputation.

IT will always be my Pride, that I have printed an impartial and truly independent Newspaper, and that I have done my Endeavours, humble and limited as they have been, to rescue my Countrymen from the darkness of Ignorance, and to awaken Them to a Sense of their Privileges as Human Beings, and, as such, of their Importance in the grand scale of Creation. That I have intended well, however inadequate my Exertions have been to my Wishes, will be a Consolation to me when far removed from the many friendly and dear connections I have formed in this Country. Filled with every kind Sentiment toward those who wish otherwise, I bid Farewell to my numerous and steady Friends; and grateful for every part FAVOUR, whether continued to the present Moment, or withdrawn from Political Motives, I remain wishing every HONEST MAN, whatever his Political or Religious Sentiments may be, Health, Peace, and Comfort.

JOSEPH GALES

6.

James Montgomery;
Editorial

Sheffield Iris No 1
4 July 1794

Within a month of the *Sheffield Register's* final instalment a new paper appeared on the Sheffield high street. Founded by James Montgomery (with the help of Unitarian minister James Naylor) this new paper was called the *Sheffield Iris.* This, the paper's first editorial, works hard to pitch itself as a worthy successor to the *Register* whilst also distancing itself from that paper's overtly radical tone. The front page boasted a new motto, 'Ours are the plans of fair, delightful peace, unwarped by party rage to live like brothers', presenting the paper as a far less polemic proposition than its controversial predecessor.

The editors of this paper beg leave to assure the public, that every endeavour will be used to render it worthy of their patronage; and if a careful selection of the earliest intelligence can recommend it to their favour, they doubt not of its being honoured with liberal support. They profess themselves desirous to avoid, in this publication, the influence of party spirit. Like other men, they have their own political opinions and their own political attachments; and they have no scruple to declare themselves friends to the cause of Peace and Reform, however such a declaration may be likely to expose them in the present time of alarm to obnoxious epithets and unjust and ungenerous reproaches. But while they acknowledge themselves unconvinced of the necessity or expediency of the present war, and fully persuaded that a melioration of the state of the representative body is intimately connected with the true interests of the nation, they declare their firm attachment to the Constitution of its Government, as administered by KING, LORDS and COMMONS; and they scorn the imputations which would represent every reformer as a Jacobin, and every advocate of peace as an enemy of the country. They pity those persons, whatever their principles may be, who, in endeavouring to defend them, have recourse to the mean acts of vilifying and abusing their opponents; and they proclaim their own firm purpose to avoid descending to the littleness of personal controversy, or to recriminations unworthy alike of Britons, of Christians, or of men. It is their wish, on the contrary, to cherish, as far as they are able, a good opinion of those who differ from them in sentiment; to allow the weight of their arguments where they deserve consideration; to place them in the most favourable view; and to give their readers a fair opportunity of forming an impartial judgment by a comparison of the best remarks which can be made on all sides. At the same time, they declare it is not their intention to enter themselves as parties on the field of political controversy. For though they shall think it their duty to state the reasonings on both sides upon public and interesting questions, they do not conceive it to be at all the proper business of the editor of a newspaper to present his readers with his own political opinions: and whatever theirs may at any time be, it is too much their wish to live in peace and charity with all men to feel disposed to come forward as angry zealots or violent partisans. Their utmost ambition will be gratified if they shall be able to recommend this paper to the public notice as authentic, impartial, and early record of the sentiments of OTHERS, on these interesting events which almost every day now furnishes, and which cannot but mark out the present area to the peculiar attention of the politician, the historian and the philosopher.

7.

Barbara Hoole;
To the *Iris*
Sheffield Iris No 1
4 July 1794

Though during the first few months of the *Sheffield Iris* there was seen a discernible shift in style and content, poetry was to remain central to James Montgomery's project. This dedication is emphasised in the first instalment, which presents the paper's manifesto in verse.

O fay, art thou the bright ey'd maid,
Saturina's messenger confest?
Does sacred truth thy mind pervade,
And love celestial warm thy breast?

Com'st thou with covenanted bow,
Blest signature of heav'nly peace,
To lay the waves of faction low,
And bid the winds of discord cease;

The various forms of good intent
In one pure social league to bind;
By prudence taught, through virtue bent
To reconcile the public mind?

Are these aims? Bright vision, hail!
'Midst freedom's clouded hemisphere
No storms thy genius shall assail,
No latent mischiefs hover near.

Fair be thy form and gay thy hue.
In learning Tyrian lustre drest,
Grounded on Truth's celestial blue,
Ting'd from the Muse's yellow vest!

Far may thy glowing beauties shine,
And glad success secure the beam,
Whilst Reason mild and Peace divine,
Roll o'er the earth their lurid stream!

This publication has been produced by 'Sheffield: Print, Protest and Poetry, 1790–1810', a Cultural Engagement Project based in the School of English at the University of Sheffield, generously funded by the Arts and Humanities Research Council. The project is directed by Dr Hamish Mathison and researched by Dr Adam James Smith. It focuses on the collections of the *Sheffield Register* (1784–1794) and the *Sheffield Iris* (1794–1825) held in the University of Sheffield's University Library Special Collections.

The ten poems selected for this volume represent the themes and techniques of the full range of texts examined during this project. The complete anthology can be found on the project's website, supplemented by additional commentary and resources. Detailed references for sources cited in this volume can also be found there. If you enjoy the poems in this book we recommend visiting our site where you can continue reading about the inspiring (and surprising) story of James Montgomery's time as editor of the *Sheffield Iris*.

–
printprotestpoetry.group.shef.ac.uk
twitter.com/18C_ShefProtest
facebook.com/PrintProtestPoetry

The Poems

Commentaries

Essay

Poetry, Conspiracy and Radicalism in Sheffield
Edited by Hamish Mathison and Adam James Smith

Volume Editor	Matthew Cheeseman
Editorial Assistant	William Lloyd
Design	Go! Grafik, www.gografik.ch
Printing	Graphius, Deckers Snoeck nv
Edition	500 copies

printprotestpoetry.group.shef.ac.uk
twitter.com/18C_ShefProtest
facebook.com/PrintProtestPoetry

The
University
Of
Sheffield.

Arts & Humanities
Research Council